This book is to be returned on or before
the last date stamped below.

D0545803

WITHDRAWN
FROM
LEARNING RESOURCES
CENTRE

KINGSTON COLLEGE   TELEPEN
00000923

Frontispiece Misericords, St. Mary's Church, Ripple, Hereford and Worcester.
B. Clayton. Copyright Batsford. (*top*) August: Reaping. (*bottom*) October: Gathering
acorns for pig-food.

Farms in England

prehistoric to present

Peter Fowler

KINGSTON COLLEGE OF FURTHER EDUCATION LIBRARY

ROYAL COMMISSION ON HISTORICAL MONUMENTS ENGLAND

LONDON HER MAJESTY'S STATIONERY OFFICE

© Crown copyright 1983
First published 1983

ISBN 0 11 701130 4

HER MAJESTY'S STATIONERY OFFICE

Government Bookshops

49 High Holborn, London WC1V 6HB
13a Castle Street, Edinburgh EH2 3AR
Brazennose Street, Manchester M60 8AS
Southey House, Wine Street, Bristol BS1 2BQ
258 Broad Street, Birmingham B1 2HE
80 Chichester Street, Belfast BT1 4JY

*Government publications are also available
through booksellers*

ACKNOWLEDGEMENTS

Copyright of the photographs in this book is held by the National
Monuments Record unless otherwise stated.
The Commission is grateful for permission to reproduce photographs in
the National Monuments Record of which the copyright is held by:

B.T. Batsford
Butser Ancient Farm Project Trust
A.W. Everett
P. Florey
Hertford Museum
Mrs A. Keiller
The Duke of Norfolk
D.N. Medcalf
Oxfordshire County Libraries
West Air Photography
B. Wingham

The author is grateful for help from many colleagues, especially those in the
Architectural Library and Air Photographic Section of the National
Monuments Record and in the Commission's Order and Photographic
Sections. Particular expert assistance from J.T. Smith and Priscilla Boniface
is gladly acknowledged.

At HMSO, among many staff who have contributed, Richard Nelson
designed the book with skill and sympathy.

Printed in England for Her Majesty's Stationery Office
by Jolly & Barber Ltd. Rugby

Dd 717095 C60

	K.C.F.E. Library
Class No.	338.1
Acc. No.	00000923
Date Rec	10.11.88
Order No.	T2963

EDITOR'S FOREWORD

All the photographs in this book are held in the National Monuments Record (NMR), a national archive which is part of the Royal Commission on Historical Monuments (England). The NMR originated in 1941 as the National Buildings Record which, at a time when so much was being destroyed, took upon itself the task of photographing as many historic buildings as possible before it was too late. The Record continued its work after the War and was transferred to the Royal Commission in 1963. As the NMR, it now covers both architectural and archaeological subjects and contains well over a million photographs, together with maps, plans and other documents, relating to England's man-made heritage. The NMR is a public archive, open from 10.00 – 17.30 hours on weekdays; prints can be supplied to order.

This book is the fifth of a series intended to illustrate the wealth of photographic material publicly available in the NMR. Many of the photographs are valuable in their own right, either because of their age or because they are the only records we now possess of buildings, and even whole environments, which have disappeared. Unlike other Commission publications, these are primarily picture-books, drawing entirely on what happens to be in the NMR. No attempt is made to treat each subject comprehensively nor to accompany it with a deeply researched text, but the text and captions are intended to give meaning to the photographs by indicating a context within which they can be viewed. It would be pleasing if they suggested lines of enquiry for others to follow. The titles in the series show where the strengths of the archive lie. Equally, of course, the collection is weak in some respects, and I hope that many of those who see this volume may be reminded of old, and perhaps disregarded, photographs of buildings and scenes in their possession. We would be glad to be told of the whereabouts of such photographs as potential contributions to the national record.

A high proportion of the photographs in the NMR relate in one way or another to farming for the simple reason that England was a predominantly agrarian country until relatively recently. The problems of selection have therefore been formidable. While attempting to present a visually interesting view of the subject, this collection also consciously seeks to indicate the enormous range of material in the NMR illustrating the English countryside. The spread in time, from prehistory to present, ranges in one dimension; the geographical distribution from Cornwall through Kent to Northumberland extends in another; while the nature of the images themselves, created over more than a century, varies widely too.

The selection began as photographs of farm buildings. In fairness to the NMR, however, the meaning of the word 'Farms' in the title had to expand to embrace the three different senses of the word: 'farmhouse', though this is but lightly touched on here; 'farmstead', that is the assemblage of domestic and non-domestic buildings in and around the farmyard; and farm as used in the phrase 'life on the farm', meaning the farm in an extended sense including its lands, crops and stock and the people working with them.

Peter Fowler,
Secretary,
Royal Commission on
Historical Monuments (England);
General Editor,
NMR Photographic Archives

Royal Commission on Historical
Monuments (England),
Fortress House,
23 Savile Row,
London W1X 1AB

SELECT BIBLIOGRAPHY

M.W. **Barley**, *The English Farmhouse and Cottage*. Routledge, Kegan Paul. 1961

R.J. **Brown**, *English Farmhouses*. Hale. 1982

R.W. **Brunskill**, *Traditional Buildings of England*. Gollancz. 1981
   Traditional Farm Buildings of Britain. Gollancz. 1982

Gillian **Darley**, *The National Trust Book of the Farm*. Weidenfeld and Nicholson. 1981

George Ewart **Evans**, *The Farm and the Village*. Faber and Faber. 1969

H.P.R. **Finberg** (ed.), J. **Thirsk** (ed.), *The Agrarian History of England and Wales*. 8 volumes in progress, Cambridge University Press.

Edward **Hart**, *Victorian and Edwardian Farming from Old Photographs*. Batsford. 1981

Nigel **Harvey**, *A History of Farm Buildings in England and Wales*. David and Charles. 1970
   Old Farm Buildings. Shire Publications. 2nd ed. 1977
   The Industrial Archaeology of Farming in England and Wales. Batsford. 1980

T. **Hennell**, *Change in the Farm*. E.P. Publishing. 1977

W.G. **Hoskins** (ed.), *History from the Farm*. Faber and Faber. 1970

Eric **Mercer**, *English Vernacular Houses*. HMSO. 1975

Roger **Mercer** (ed.), *Farming Practice in British Prehistory*. Edinburgh University Press. 1982

C.S. and C.S. **Orwin**, *The Open Fields*. Oxford. 3rd ed. 1967

J. and J. **Penoyre**, *Houses in the Landscape*. Faber and Faber. 1978

J.E.C. **Peters**, *Discovering Traditional Farm Buildings*. Shire Publications. 1981

H.G. **Ramm**, R.W. **McDowall** and Eric **Mercer**, *Sheilings and Bastles*. HMSO. 1970

John **Weller**, *History of the Farmstead*. Faber and Faber. 1982

Gordon **Winter**, *A Country Camera 1844–1914*. Penguin. 1973

(*above*) Oxen ploughing in the Cotswolds. H.W. Taunt, *c.* 1895. Copyright
Oxfordshire County Libraries.

Farms in England

'... what farms are those?'
Housman, *The Welsh Marches*

INTRODUCTION

Farming (Plates 1-2)

Farming is a way of life; but in essence it is only a means to an end, the production of food. Food can be acquired either from the wild, or produced domestically. Catching or collecting wild food long ago ceased to be a significant way for England to feed itself; subsistence, self-sufficient and then commercial farming have in turn developed.

Food from the farm comes in two distinct, though related, ways: from plant crops grown for human consumption, and from animals. This fundamental distinction between arable and pastoral farming, between crop and stock husbandry (*1,2*)*, is deeply embedded in our human consciousness: the story of Cain and Abel, respectively arable and stock farmers, is the Biblical version of it.

Man the farmer is in fact a relatively late arrival on the human scene. He was domesticating plants and animals around the eastern Mediterranean during the period 10000–5000 BC; farming communities were present in western Europe, including the British Isles, during the two millennia 5000–3000 BC. Farming has only existed for some ten thousand years after many hundreds of thousands of years when Man survived without it.

*Numbers *1–97* in brackets in the text refer to the numbers of the Plates.

Farms (Plates 3–10)

Little visible evidence in the way of farming landscapes or structures remains in England from the early millennia of British agriculture. A number of what appear to have been important communal sites of the early farming communities of the fourth millennium are nevertheless known (*3*). After *c.* 2000 BC the variety and extent of our information improve. Over tracts of higher land like Bodmin Moor, Cornwall (*4*), the main elements of farming landscapes of the second millennium survive physically in considerable completeness. Fields, farms, buildings, tracks, boundaries, sometimes laid out in a planned arrangement of enclosure which was not to be seen again in the English countryside for nearly four thousand years, spread impressively over tracts of countryside supposedly 'natural' in its beauty to twentieth-century eyes. Much of such higher farmland was abandoned as the climate deteriorated in the centuries around 1000 BC, but the landscape in general filled up with farming communities during later prehistoric times and the Roman period (*5*). Though much of the evidence they created has been unknowingly flattened by later farmers, the English countryside is packed with the buried remains of fields and farms.

Existing farms in their landscapes show enormous variety. In part this derives from the local environment, in part from history, and in part from the type of farming being practised. The typical situation in lowland England (6) is for a farm to lie in a village grouped closely around a church and surrounded by its fields. Usually this is a medieval arrangement which has persisted, though the origins may well be much earlier. Elsewhere, and particularly in the west and north of England, farms occur singly or in hamlets, whether they lie on a valley bottom or up in the hills (7,8). And, contrary to common belief, it is in the north rather than in the south that the characteristic form of the English village around a green occurs (9). Many of these, and indeed of other types, suggest that far from being a natural organic growth, they have at some time been planned. Villages with farms, and indeed farms themselves, can expand and shrink and move around the landscape. Contemporary pictorial evidence (10), particularly from late medieval times onwards, seldom shows a static scene.

The farmhouse (Plates 11-22)

Architecturally, farmhouses vary across the English landscape; the enormous regional diversity reflects different histories, societies, building materials and types of farming. Ownership is crucial too: was a farmhouse owner-occupied or lived in by a tenant?

In the far north of England, for example, three aspects of farming there can be inferred from the archaeology of some farmhouses. The dominance of pastoral farming on the hills is strongly suggested by the repeating linear arrangement of house/barn/byre in a single range of buildings set along or up and down the hillside (11). A fundamental aspect of farming practice in Cumbrian society until recently was 'transhumance', reflected in the often stone-built but nevertheless temporarily occupied sheilings whose ruins characterize the fells (12). Along the Anglo-Scottish border, at least until three centuries ago, warfare and an absence of central authority were significant local factors. The local farmhouses, especially in north Northumberland, reflect these facts of daily life

by adopting in the 16th and 17th centuries the unique form of a bastle, a type of building which afforded rapid protection to both stock and inhabitants (13).

The thatched timber and mud farmhouse of southern England is a type which certainly has origins deep in prehistoric times (14). In the first millennium BC, large round houses up to nearly 60 feet (18m) in diameter must have dominated many farming settlements. Their Roman equivalent, at least socially, was surely the villa; and even though show-piece villas, like Chedworth (15), look so completely different, *functionally* they were similar. They were the centre of a farm and included a house. Furthermore, excavation has shown several to have begun life before the Roman Conquest in the timber and thatch tradition of prehistory.

England contains many farmhouses of medieval times and is remarkably rich in those of the 16th to the 19th centuries; and as farmhouses abound, so do photographs of them. The four reproduced here (16-19) can only be general indicators of the material in the field and in the archive.

Farmhouses, whatever their architectural interest or value as historical evidence, were built for people to live in, and they have been moulded by those human lives. Put relevant people in front of or inside one, even if only for photographic purposes, and the record leaps to life. A farmhouse and its people, captured before the shooting at the high noon of Victorian order (20); one man and his pipe, his peace and a roomful of memories over 345 years (21) – these two scenes with people in them say more than, and in a different way from, photographs of buildings on their own. With or without people, however, the farmhouse of whatever date or type can best be understood not singly but in the context of the farm, its farmyard and its countryside (22).

The farmyard (Plates 23-49)

Yards are for some the most interesting parts

of farms; yet, although that interest comes in part from the apparent disorder and an expectation of the unexpected round the corner, farmyards are purposeful places the elements of which are fairly predictable. It is in their scale and internal patterning, and in the shapes and materials of their individual buildings, that variety appears, from yard to yard and mile to mile across the countryside.

Impressive farmyards occur in many parts of England; a certain grandeur often stems from the presence of one or more huge barns. The best-known type is the tithe barn (23), sometimes standing alone but often in a farmyard with other buildings such as a granary. Large barns, representing as they did a long-term capital investment, characteristically also incorporate the major building materials in any given area: limestone in the Cotswolds, for example, or timber and thatch in East Anglia (24).

Barns were multi-purpose buildings. They were primarily used, of course, to hold the harvest, often cereal but they were also places of work and, sometimes, play. Animals, too, were housed in them at times. While outstanding examples of the type could in places provide an appropriate farmyard background to equally magnificent animals (25), the general run of storage buildings, of livestock and of crop-processing did not always attain such a rustic grandeur (26). Some local building materials too did not permit architectural exuberance, though their interest to the modern historian of the vernacular building tradition is no less great (27). Cob, for example, a mixture of mud, marl, chalk or gravel with dung and some binding material such as hair or straw, was frequently used.

Many of England's prehistoric farms were built of such potentially transient material. Then, as later, wattle-and-daub was a favourite material for filling the spaces between the upright timbers of a wooden-framed building. The appearance of dilapidation contrived in a modern reconstruction of an Iron Age farmstead may convey past reality but not necessarily so (28, 29, cf. 14). Nevertheless, there appears to be all the difference in the world between such assumed prehistoric squalor and the architectural grandeur of a planned, relatively recent farm; but, just as the similarities in farming terms are significant in comparing prehistoric farm and Roman villa (14,15,50), functionally there is very little difference between Little Woodbury as imagined and Brandon and Byshottles in fact (30).

Despite many an imposing farmhouse and splendid barn, the English farmstead is seldom deliberately pretentious. The scarcity of architectural gateways into farmyards bears this out. Some which survive may have been entrances to grand houses or ecclesiastical establishments rather than just to farms (31). A gateway could be made into something useful as well as impressive: a pigeon house, for example, was a very convenient function for the empty, upper spaces (32). Entrances were certainly built to impress at some of the planned farms of the later 18th and 19th centuries (33); yet the barred gate remains the characteristic entrance to the typical farmyard (34).

Old-fashioned farmyards like that have become rare but not very long ago such scenes were normal. A variety of wooden-wheeled vehicles and pieces of wooden farmyard furniture, such as a trough, were commonplace (35). It now requires a photograph more than one hundred years old (36) to give a glimpse of that wooden, higgledy-piggledy yet ordered reality of shape and space, of that pleasing irregularity of line and angle which no tidy-minded modern farmer will, understandably, tolerate. The change in attitude was symbolized by a new type of farm in the first half of the 19th century. Then, many a 'model' farm was deliberately built, often to be as much an inspiration to other farmers as to serve the immediate needs of its owner. At worst, these new farmsteads degenerated into an uninspiring functionalism; but, at best, where a happy marriage of architectural style and farming efficiency was achieved, they could be splendid.

In their attention to detail they were particularly impressive, successfully tackling basic problems of water supply and effluent disposal while attending to pleasing matters of ornament (37-9).

Water supply has always been a problem. The distribution of water around a farm continued to be a major drain on a farm's resources, particularly in the days of the steam ploughs. The traction engines needed enormous quantities of water. While cattle could be taken to the familiar farmyard pond (40), machines had to be supplied with water out in the fields (41). Meanwhile, for domestic purposes in the farmyard, the application of a little science to produce the hand-pump (42) reduced the many dreary hours that the 'hands' had once had to spend in winding buckets of water up from a well.

The other principal liquids to be catered for in the farmyard depended to a large extent on the type of farming practised, and this of course largely depended on the area where the farm was located. On some cattle farms, for example, the traditional milking shed or shippon was replaced by the purpose-built dairy (43), as much to improve the health of the cows as the hygiene with which the milk and its products were handled. In other places, different varieties of alcoholic drink were produced. Cider from Somerset and Herefordshire is perhaps one of the best known: its production involved the annual use of some very heavy machinery indeed (44). And every day, all year round, the farmyard witnessed the many humble but essential tasks which together ensured that the farming life continued with at least a modicum of comfort. Chopping wood, for example, was a task known to practically everyone on a farm until very recently (45). It is difficult now to envisage the sheer amount of wood that lay around in farmyards and the constant use of it.

The farmyard was the working centre of the farm. Whether it was on an arable farm with its great barns, its expanses of thatch, tile or barge board, with its horses, wagons and acres of straw (46), or whether it was on a pasture farm, practically everything came sooner or later to the farmyard. Threshing, when it became a complicated operation with several machines, was more often than not carried out in the farmstead's rickyard rather than out in the fields (47); and it was to the farmyard with its barns and shelter sheds that the tractor came when it supplanted the horse as the main traction power on the farm (48). The new types of plough that the tractor could pull and, later, the whole array of new machinery which developed when steam, electricity and then the internal combustion engine were used in farming (49), threatened to take over the farmyard. The new machines fitted, sometimes awkwardly and sometimes all too conveniently, into buildings and spaces which had been designed, often hundreds of years earlier, for other days and other ways.

Crops on the farm (Plates 50-74)

The barn is the most characteristic farm building associated with crops. Barns, most now gone, must have existed in their thousands through-out prehistoric and historic times, many of them quite small buildings built entirely of organic materials (50).

Barns are often difficult to date (51-3). Sometimes they are blessed with datestones and occasionally they are even more securely dated (54). They tended to have other buildings added to and around them. The angle between the nave and the porch could, for example, easily be infilled with a useful shed; the gable wall could easily be used as one end of a granary or implement shed (55).

Barns, though primarily built for crop storage, were also closely associated with animals (56). Essential tasks could be carried out under cover. Threshing with a flail was the traditional job carried out in the space between the opposed pair of barn doors (57), a manual task super-seded in the mid-19th century by the application of steam-driven power on many farms. The

stationary engine which could be so conveniently manoeuvred into position to do its job
then (58) carried out many of the tasks now
performed by electric-powered machines and
tractors.

Though several barns have been carefully
preserved and sometimes restored, numerous
lesser ones are now threatened by the dilapidation which has overtaken many earlier
examples. At moments in this sad process,
however, the skeleton of a barn can reveal
intimate details of its structure and of the
craftsmanship with which it was built (59).
When fully maintained, in contrast, such
structures can be truly impressive inside,
looking for all the world like the agrarian
versions of the large contemporary parish
churches (60).

In the north and west, stone barns, though
not as large as the largest in the south, perhaps
convey an even greater air of permanence (61).
Again they often enclose a building for several
purposes – to milk cows, shelter calves, keep
equipment and to store grain and hay in a first-
floor loft. Brick too can be as excellent a material
for intentionally long-term, multi-purpose farm
buildings as it is for many farmhouses, a
distinction that becomes blurred when the barn
itself is provided with the appropriate fittings,
such as a chimney (62), for human occupation.

Not every barn that we see today was
originally built as such. The need for these
dominant and purposeful buildings was so
great that they tend to have been carved out of
other large buildings when opportunity arose.
That opportunity occurred, above all, after the
Dissolution: the close physical connection
between church and farm is illustrated by the
farm at Littlemore (22) and by the conversion to
barns of a chapel at Church Farm, Ruxley (46),
and of the Priory Church at Latton, Essex (63).

Barns, like other types of building, produce
their own oddities. An unwalled but thatched
structure standing on top of staddle-stones, for
example, could clearly be used for the same
purpose as a more normal-looking barn (64).

Nor are all granaries obvious to the eye: a
Norfolk version above a wherry arch is a particular local adaptation in a grain-producing area
with many windmills and slow streams (65).

Around and outside the farmstead lie many
buildings connected with crop-production. In
the days of the modern corn-dryer, the corn-
drying kiln in the fields has disappeared
altogether; but not so long ago and certainly in
medieval times, it was essential (66). Cereals
had to be dried in order to be stored for human
consumption; in contrast, grasses and other
cattle food were stored green to make better
silage (67). Among various other buildings for
storing, drying or processing field-crops, the
oast house (68) is the most obvious example.

The main types of farm buildings have
tended to be long-lived. We see little change,
for example, between the types represented on
Chauncey's drawings of about 1700 (69,70),
those we know to have existed in 1500 and
those we see on photographs of 1900. The mill
is a case in point. Crucial to farming, it used to
be one of the most important buildings in the
English countryside, for only there could the
farmer change his cereal crop into something
which he could sell for others to eat. This
applied whether the mill was driven by water or
wind (71,72). Chronologically between such
natural and cheap power-sources and today's
machines, another source of energy was tapped:
in the 19th century many a farmer fitted to his
barn a wheel-house in which an animal, usually
a horse, plodded round and round transmitting
power through a shaft to a piece of machinery
inside the barn itself (73). Nevertheless, a
machine has not readily been devised to replace
the hand in some tasks: until recently potato-
planting was one of these (74).

Livestock on the farm (Plates 75–95)

The needs of livestock also created a need for
particular types of farm building. Just as the
barn could be used for animals as well as crop
storage, so many a cattle shelter has a hayloft or

other storage room above it (*75*). Nevertheless, the inside of a cow-house, byre or stable is quite different from a barn's interior; the needs to divide the animals, provide for their food and clean them out all produce a distinctive array of internal fittings and fixtures (*76*). In certain circumstances the exterior is quite distinctive too, though pigsties carved in the living rock are not very common (*77*). More familiar as the place where animals live is the manure-deep farmyard accumulated from cows and rooted over by pigs (*78*). Purpose-built stables can also be easily recognizable though they are not always among the most outstanding examples of architecture (*79*). In contrast, a rare example of a stylish and interesting stable is preserved in a fine Tudor building in Essex (*80*).

Like arable farming, livestock husbandry has its particular rituals and magic. The hagstone hung over a stall to ward evil away from the horse is a long-lived and potent symbol (*81*); similarly, a rich folklore is associated with the blacksmith and his activities (*82*). Shepherding, however, although equally endowed with its own mystique, tends not to have created solid buildings like stables, byres and barns. Rather it has been an outdoor activity in which man has gone to the flock rather than brought it to the farmstead. Nevertheless, structures were required: shepherds erected many yards of hurdling in folding their flocks on the plough-land (*83*); and at lambing, dipping (*2*) and shearing times they lived for weeks on end in those rather uncomfortable-looking wheeled but unsprung huts which used to be such a familiar sight on the southern English Downs (*84*). Even at one of the very centres of the woollen industry, Witney, the buildings directly associated with shearing are still somewhat insubstantial (*85*).

Farmers in England have always had to provide food for their stock during the winter. In mixed or pastoral farming the hay crop was just as important to the livestock farmer as was the production of cereal to his counterpart on the arable farm. In medieval times, the same system of allocation of crop was used in the meadows as is more familiar to us in the strips of the common arable fields. A remarkable survival of this persisted into this century at Yarnton, Oxfordshire (*86*). For millennia before, 'the grassy harvest of the river-fields' had been cut with a scythe (*87*). Some of it went indoors to hay-lofts (*27,32,36,75*), some to stacks in the farmstead (*26,69*), and some to stacks thatched with straw out in the fields (*88*).

All sorts of 'livestock' other than the familiar cow, horse, sheep, pig, dog and cat were commonly kept on farms until quite recently. Incredible though it may seem to the modern farmer, the rabbit, for example, was deliberately cultivated as a living larder for the winters when fresh meat was short (*89*). Similarly, bees and various birds animated the farmyard: ducks and geese, hens for eggs (*23*), cocks for sport (*90*) and pigeons as the feathered counterpart of the rabbit. As a result of the last, dovecotes are among the more familiar, 'folksy' buildings dotted around England, out in the fields (*22,91,92*), as ornate features of the farmyard (*32,69,93*), and fixed on walls (*71*). They ranged enormously in size and external design (*94*); their interiors, though also variable, basically consisted of tiers of cubby-holes in which the birds could nest, lay and coo (*95*).

Farms in the landscape (Plates 96, 97).

The English farm and its landscape vary enormously from region to region and have done so through time. Compare a farm and its setting on the edge of the silt fens in Lincolnshire with one on the edge of Dartmoor and striking differences are apparent. Yet the similarities are also striking. Perhaps the most significant is the antiquity perceptible in these different landscapes, regardless of geology and relief. Buried, on the surface as visible archaeological evidence and still alive in the types and patterns of buildings, of farmsteads and of former land arrangements, a cultural continuity of some sort seems crammed into these acres, farmed and fashioned from prehistory to present.

FARMS IN CONTEXT

1 HARVESTING, FORTHAMPTON, GLOUCESTERSHIRE
The crop-producing farm in its motorless heyday at harvest-time in the mid-19th century. Apparently little had changed since 1290: 'At reaping time . . . the hayward should have his workers assemble and hasten to send their sickles into the corn and he should make them reap in orderly fashion . . . and the shocks set up in good order so that they may dry the sooner and be conveniently and evenly tied up in small sheaves, for a small sheaf is handier than a large one to cart to rick and to thresh . . ..' *Fleta, c.* 1290. Other stages in crop-production are illustrated facing page 1 and in Pls. 47-9, 57, 58, 64 and 71-3. Photographer unknown, *c.* 1865.

2 SHEEPWASHING, RADCOT, OXFORDSHIRE
For early farmers of domesticated animals, the sheep was primarily a source of milk but the wealth accumulated in East Anglia and the Cotswolds in medieval England was gathered from the fleece. A happy clothier remarked at the time: 'I thank God and ever shall It was the sheep that payed for all.' While it may look as though the eight men in the photograph are busy drowning the sheep, they are in fact 'dipping' them to launder them, probably in early spring. A Second World War block-house now occupies the site but the cut in the bank of the River Isis remains. H.W. Taunt, *c.* 1890. Copyright Oxfordshire County Libraries.

3 THE TRUNDLE, GOODWOOD, WEST SUSSEX

'... these chance hieroglyphs scored by men on the surface of the hills.' W.H. Hudson, *A Shepherd's Life*

The early farmers of England have left behind two main types of monument. The best-known are their burial places, long mounds often with stone chambers and surrounding walls in rocky areas. These farmers also built what we call 'causewayed enclosures', places where they apparently assembled and probably traded the products of their farming.

On the edge of Goodwood racecourse (*top left*) lies The Trundle, a strongly fortified place of the last centuries BC: inside its ramparts, and flattened by that later use, the two roughly concentric boundaries of a Neolithic causewayed enclosure, probably built *c.* 4000 BC, show clearly on this air photograph. NMR, 1977.

4 LESKERNICK HILL, BODMIN MOOR, CORNWALL
From about 2000 BC, visible evidence of prehistoric farmers in the present landscape becomes more widespread, particularly on the higher, now-marginal uplands of the west and the north where later farmers have not disturbed the remains. Bodmin Moor is a classic example: a flourishing agricultural area in the second millennium BC, much of its surface is covered, as on this air photograph, with stone-walled fields with their contemporary farming settlements (*right, centre*, with seven round houses in the centre) and isolated buildings (*bottom left*, two). NMR, 1979.

5 RAINHAM, HAVERING, GREATER LONDON

'PALIMPSEST n. Writing material or manuscript on which the original writing has been effaced to make room for a second writing.' *Concise Oxford Dictionary*, 6th ed., 1976.

In contrast to the uplands, much of lowland England does not appear to carry evidence of prehistoric farming. In fact, it is extensively covered by old, farming landscapes rather than just being dotted with the occasional archaeological site.

This vertical air photograph of crop-marks – the usually darker marks often produced best in cereal crops just before harvest – is typical. It shows in plan a whole complex of prehistoric and Romano-British features cutting and super-imposed on each other in a gravel subsoil in one part of one modern field. A probably Roman field system with a ditched roadway (*bottom right*) appears to be closely related to the late-prehistoric enclosure so sharply defined by the three concentric dark lines marking its ditches. The black dot in its right corner is a well. Excavation has shown at least three other settlements and a cremation cemetery to exist amongst this complex, so characteristic of England's arable farmlands. NMR, 1976.

6 (*opposite, below*) BRAYBROOKE,
NORTHAMPTONSHIRE
A village in profile, representing the typical
English settlement of farms and houses grouped
around the medieval parish church protruding
from its cluster of 'immemorial elms'. Though the
view recalls Belloc's sentiments about 'living in
the Midlands, that are sodden and unkind', here
the medieval ponds not only held fish but, as the
saw-edged water-line on the left clearly shows,
were also ploughed. RCHM, 1970s.

7 FARMSTEAD, NEAR TIVERTON, DEVON
The single farmstead, typical of the west and
north of England, contrasts with the nucleated
village of the Midlands (Pl. 6). This example,
situated close to a river but lying just above the
flood-plain, characteristically nestles in a fold in
the hills and also shows on a small scale a familiar
development from the core of older buildings –
house, byre and shed, all thatched. W. Peach, 1925.

8 GOOSEMIRE, MARDALE, SHAP RURAL, CUMBRIA
'The dwelling-houses, and contiguous outhouses, are . . . of the colour of the native rock, out of which they have
been built.' W. Wordsworth, *Guide to the Lakes*
  In a starker version of the preceding Devon farm, here stone and slate dominate what appears to be an isolated
upland farmhouse looking on to its byre (with a characteristic 1930s new roof of corrugated iron) to the north east
(*right*) and its crowstepped gabled barn to the south east. The farmstead was part of a hamlet scattered around
Mardale parish church and the Dun Bull Inn. All of it was demolished soon after this record was made, before
being drowned as Manchester's Haweswater Reservoir backed up the valley from the right to the 800-foot
contour more or less at the spot from which this photograph was taken. The very top of Wood Howe, in the
middle distance, is still just above the waters. RCHM, 2 March, 1935.

9 OLD BYLAND, NORTH YORKSHIRE

'**Byland, Old,** par., N.R. Yorks, on r. Rye, 4½m.
NW. of Hemsley, 2738 ac., pop. 123.'

Bartholomews' *Gazetteer of the British Isles*,
9th ed., 1943, reprinted 1972 'with Summery
(*sic*) of the 1971 Census'.

A planned village, like many others north of
it, with farms, buildings and houses arranged
fairly regularly around an oblong, north-south
green. Here the church, All Saints, is at the
north-east (*bottom left*) corner, behind the large
farm on its north and the houses fronting on to
the east side of the green. At the south-east
corner is Old Byland Hall and to the south-west,
across the 100 feet drop of Hill Gill, the
Grange. The Chapel and the school lie on the
west of the green, their plots running through to
the symmetrical back lane. West of that,
earthworks in the fields suggest earlier arrangements of buildings while the little curve in the
wall to their south, and west of the last farm
building, marks the site of the village animal
pound. Modern farming is seen diagonally
opposite (*bottom left*) in the expanse of roof and
the assembly of giant round bales. NMR, 1979.

10 LAXTON, NOTTINGHAMSHIRE

'. . . no other village has retained its manorial
machinery to remind us of the time when
England was a mosaic of little self-governing
republics . . .' J.D. Chambers,

Laxton: The Last English Open Field Village

The farm in the village, and the village in its
agricultural setting, are epitomized here on an
early-17th-century map in visual terms similar to
those on the preceding, modern air photograph.
The settlement layout is clear, with church to one
end and properties disposed around a T-shaped
road junction. The tree-lined (oaks rather than
elms?) boundary hedge separates settlement
from fields where strips in furlongs butt against
each other. Activities in the fields – ploughing,
sowing and harrowing – and outlying structures
of the farm like the windmill, are topics to which
we return. Extract from a *Surveye* of 1635, now in
the Bodleian Library, Oxford.

THE FARMHOUSE

11 DALE FOOT FARM, BISHOPDALE, NORTH YORKSHIRE

A characteristic example of one of the many varieties of farmhouse is illustrated by what could be called a 'linear farmstead'. The type consists of a range of buildings, often built along the side of a valley. Here the farmhouse, with a date of 1640 on the lintel over its front door, is at the far end of a line of four different buildings – probably a stable with a loft approached by outside stairs which also give into the upstairs of the next building, a shed, next to which is a waggon shed with loft and a byre with hay loft above.

The whole range faces north-west on a steep slope overlooking Bishopdale Beck in an arrangement repeated many times in the northern English landscape. NMR, 1973.

12 SHEILING GROUP, OUSBY FELL, CUMBRIA

'Here every way round about in the *wasts* as they tearme them you mey see as it were the ancient *Nomades*, a martiall kinde of men, who from the moneth of Aprill unto August, lye out scattering and summering (as they tearme it) with their cattell in little cottages here and there which they call *Sheales* and *Shealings*.' Camden (1610).

Lying at the junction of Bulman Cleugh and Black Burn some 4 miles south-west of Alston, this group of six ruined huts alone in a majestic northern landscape almost certainly consists of those referred to in 1747 as 'some old *shields*, where in former ages the people had resorted like the Asiatic Tartars, to graze their cattle in summer, a practice now quite disus'd.'

The roofed building, partly restored and the largest, has two rooms 12 feet 6 inches wide and respectively 4 feet and 8 feet 9 inches deep; the other five buildings are of different sizes but lie parallel to the stream. Together the summer houses of transhuming pastoral farmers, they represent the end of a way of farming which was once common in England but has now disappeared. RCHM, 1966.

13 (*inset*) BASTLE, BLACK MIDDENS, TARSET, NORTHUMBERLAND

The bastle was a distinctively northern farmhouse, very much confined to the Scottish borders. It was a defensible structure for men and cattle. In this example, the livestock entered the ground floor through the now partly blocked door in the east gable while people went to the first floor by way of the outside steps on the south side. The ground-floor doorways and the roof are later but the small windows are original. They lit an upper room with a wooden floor and a fireplace at the west end. RCHM, 1964.

14 'PIMPERNE HOUSE', DEMONSTRATION AREA, BUTSER ANCIENT FARM, NEAR PETERSFIELD, HAMPSHIRE

Within a few yards of the main A3 road between London and Portsmouth, where it passes through the Queen Elizabeth Country Park, sits this impressive reconstruction of a farmhouse of *c.* 300 BC. Its ground plan and its conjectural superstructure are based on the archaeological evidence excavated from an Early Iron Age settlement at Pimperne, Dorset. The round house is 42 feet in diameter and 36 feet high; its floor area is 1600 square feet beneath a roof of *c.* 16 tonnes supported by the timbers from some 200 trees.

Though some detail is obviously uncertain, the house in general gives the lie to the myth that the Ancient Britons were primitive wretches only living lives of miserable squalor. Copyright Butser Ancient Farm Project Trust, *c.* 1978.

15 ROMAN VILLA, CHEDWORTH, GLOUCESTERSHIRE

The villa was discovered by a rabbiting party in 1864. Disregard the modern custodian's house and museum in the centre of the photograph which some visitors mistake for the villa proper. The rather less obvious remains of the villa, incompletely protected by roofing, stretch in a partly uncovered, rectilinear arrangement of rooms around at least two courtyards. The museum straddles the exit from the uppermost one.

The northern range (from *bottom right* to the *nymphaeum, centre top*) stretches for some 120 yards; the villa wings enclose at least 2 acres, but the eastern limits are undefined. Structural development of the buildings ranged from the early 2nd century to the late 4th century. The villa can be envisaged as the centre of a farm during those three hundred years. B. Wingham, undated. Copyright B. Wingham.

16 POPLARS FARMHOUSE, BRETTENHAM, SUFFOLK

'To the question, what shall we do to be saved in this World?, there is no other answer but this, Look to your Moat.' Marquis of Halifax

This farmhouse of the 15th century represents two trends in domestic building in late medieval times – the continuation, after it strictly had ceased to be necessary for military purposes, of the quasi-defensive moat, now more a status symbol or ornamental feature despite the quotation; and the development of large domestic buildings. F.J. Palmer, 1963.

17 CROSSWAYS FARM, ABINGER, SURREY
A farmhouse traditionally needed a large hall-kitchen to accommodate the farmhands, but as wage-labour became more common, the need for such rooms dwindled. Everything of a service or office nature could therefore be put at the rear of the house. This development, creating the possibility of symmetrical elevations, coincided with the increasing tendency of men to separate themselves from social inferiors while copying the classes above. Crossways Farm is a clear and early example illustrating such changes in the mid-17th century. By the mid-18th century, when farmhouses had often become mere residences, the elevations of many of them could just as well have appeared in a town (*cf.* pl.18). RCHM, 1974.

18 TOP FARM, CLEEVE PRIOR, HEREFORD AND WORCESTER
A typical example of a good, mid/late-18th-century farmhouse, very *à la mode* when it appeared on the village street and doubtless built by a man out to impress as the age of the great improvers in English farming developed its momentum and its fashions. RCHM, 1973.

19 BRACKENHURST FARMHOUSE, YOXALL, STAFFORDSHIRE
Two generations later, the mid-19th-century farmhouse came to be almost standardized, at least in external appearance – and not too different from the Victorian vicarage, which was perhaps the point. Often, as here, it formed the centre-piece of a planned farmstead with a farmyard enclosed on one side by a large barn (*background*). The whole lies away from a village surrounded by its own fields. RCHM, 1966.

20 (*previous spread*) RECTORY FARM,
NORTHMOOR, OXFORDSHIRE
'Eye Nature's walks, shoot folly as it flies,
And catch the manners living as they rise'.

Pope, An Essay on Man

The north elevation of this fine 16th-century
farmhouse, altered in 1629, has hardly changed
today, eighty years after the camera clicked; yet
the country-house shooting party, though dated
by its clothes, speaks of an older order familiar
to the poet Robert Bloomfield a century earlier
when he wrote of 'The social plan That rank to
rank cements, as man to man'. Photographer
unknown, *c.* 1900. Copyright P. Florey.

21 NETHER HALL FARM, HUDDERSFIELD,
WEST YORKSHIRE
'The work is done; no more to man is given;
The grateful Farmer trusts the rest to Heaven.'

Robert Bloomfield, The Farmer's Boy

Blessed is the farmer who can sit at peace
beside his hearth dated ten years before the
Long Parliament. RCHM, 1976.

22 MINCHERY FARM, LITTLEMORE, OXFORDSHIRE
An 18th-century sketched profile of a farm in a truly bucolic scene puts the farmhouse in its context within the
farmstead. Here the site is one of particular interest and complexity since it is mixed up with the ruins of a small
Benedictine nunnery, dissolved in 1525. The barn, cart-house, outhouse, gateways and pigeon house, shown here
in such detail over a century before our first photographs, are among the basic features of the farm which the
camera explores in the next sections; but it can rarely glimpse the daily, human tasks exemplified here by the
swineherd and the lady with the ducks. H. Taunt, *c.* 1907. Copyright Oxfordshire County Libraries.

THE FARMYARD

23 BARTON FARM, BRADFORD ON AVON, WILTSHIRE

'The gates are mine to open,
As the gates are mine to close'.
    Kipling, *Our Lady of the Snow*

   Gentility moves into the farmyard through the open, welcoming, double-leaf gate, pausing with studied interest to gaze intently at some very ordinary pullets.

   In the background is one of the finest farm buildings surviving from medieval times, the 14th-century tithe barn of 'the richest nunnery in England', Shaftesbury Abbey, Dorset, which also owned the barn at Place Farm, Tisbury, Wiltshire, the largest barn in England. The barn is 168 ft. long. Opposite its south end, the granary forms one side of the yard (*left*). Its upper floor is supported on stone columns and approached by the external steps. Few farmyards can match the magnificence of this grange. Photographer unknown, *c.* 1890.

24 COLVILLE HALL, WHITE RODING, ESSEX
Overlooked by the Hall itself (*upper left*), the yard
here rivals Bradford's Barton Farm for it contains
a fine agglomeration of individually superb
buildings. The timber and thatch dominate the
scene as much as did the oolite masonry at
Bradford. Behind the 15th-century hip-roofed
granary, to the left of the track here, stretches
another of England's great medieval barns, eight
bays long and perhaps 800 years old. G.N. Kent,
1948.

25 ST AYLOTTS, SAFFRON WALDEN, ESSEX
Though clearly a photographic 'study', if not
actually posed, this scene reflects the early
morning activity in the farmyard before the
tractor triumphed. Here we glimpse in a
photograph the contemporary world captured in
words, just in time, by George Ewart Evans in *The
Horse in the Furrow* and other books. Interestingly,
the horses appear to have been stabled in the
three-strayed, 17th-century barn of which the
thatch roof seems to be under repair. The horses
themselves are in full harness, being led out to
implements already in the fields in a processional
order determined by the rank of the horsemen.
Photographer unknown, 1925. Copyright D.N.
Medcalf.

26 'COUNTRY LIFE – HAYCART GROUP'

The title is the photographer's, and clearly the action is posed or at least 'frozen'. Nevertheless, the scene takes us from the grandness of the last three plates to a more humble farmyard with a not particularly magnificent horse, an ordinary two-wheeled cart, wooden tools and the simple farming task of bringing in the hay. Presumably the month is June; presumably the *dramatis personae* are trying to make a rick. Three may be genuinely at work but the shiny shoes, better clothes and general demeanour of the two young gents in the foreground suggest that the farmyard may not have been their usual habitat. H.W. Taunt, *c.* 1900. Copyright Oxfordshire County Libraries.

27 LANGDALE FARM, WIDECOMBE, DEVON

Farmyards vary enormously from one part of the country to another. Local characteristics here are the mixture of building materials in the granary on the right – cob and thatch, stone, presumably granite, for the steps, bricks for patching, and wood to prop it up. Behind is another long barn of cob and thatch, while to the left is a building typical of West of England cattle farming, a byre below with an open-fronted hay loft, or tallet, above. The presence of the midden in the foreground shows that this yard, despite appearances, is working properly at least in producing manure for the fields, one of the most important functions of a farmyard. E.M. Gardner, 1949.

LITTLE WOODBURY, BRITFORD, WILTSHIRE

The improbable-sounding name for what was to become a famous archaeological site just outside Salisbury was invented for the features on Pl. 28 in juxtaposition to the already-known and properly named Great Woodbury just a few yards away. The dark-lined enclosure surrounds a late-prehistoric farm containing, as the air photograph shows, a large black feature and lots of dots. The former turned out to be, on excavation in the 1930s, working areas in the farmyard where the chalk had been disturbed; the latter proved to be pits, often about 6 feet deep, in which grain had been stored and into which rubbish had finally been tipped. What the air photograph does not show, however, are the smaller holes made by posts for buildings and other structures; such were nevertheless found when a wide strip was excavated through the site and out across the entrance clearly visible at the bottom.

In an attempt to interest the British people in their history in the gloom of the post-war world, the Central Office of Information made a film for which they reconstructed, with expert advice, part of the Little Woodbury settlement. Much of what is seen in Pl. 29 remains controversial but the scene does not look quite so odd when it is realized that the reconstruction is much less than full-size. The heap in the middle is the main house (compare Pl. 14).

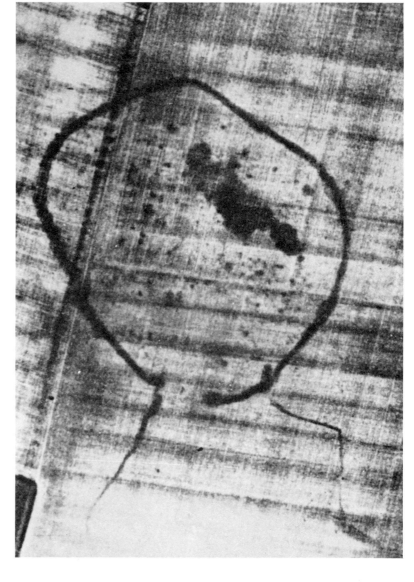

28 Vertical air photograph, showing Little Woodbury as a cropmark. A. Keiller, early 1930s.

29 Reconstruction of part of Little Woodbury as it was thought in 1945 that it might have been about 300 BC. Photographer unknown.

30 HOME FARM, BRANDON AND
BYSHOTTLES, COUNTY DURHAM

The sharpness, the scale, the cleanliness and the
order of this 19th-century model farm contrast
with Little Woodbury and indeed the other
farmyards so far illustrated. Here, as much as
possible is stored and worked indoors in the
great building to the rear. The yard itself is
concreted, with drains and runnels to keep the
liquids moving. The pig sties across the yard
represent the height of efficiency; and the roof is
not to keep the pigs in luxury but recognizes that,
having neither fur nor hair, they require more
protection. This was the organized farm with its
systematic farmyard, modern but still dependent
on the traditional sources of power, men and
animals. NMR, 1981.

31 (*opposite*) GATEWAY, COLVILLE HALL, WHITE RODING, ESSEX

'It matters not how straight the gate'.

W.E. Henley, *Echoes*

The idea of a farm needing a proper gateway goes back to prehistory (Pls. 28, 29) and it keeps returning. This free-standing – if that is the adjective – red brick gateway, built soon after 1500, used to mark the approach to the Hall and its magnificent farmyard (Pl. 24). The surmounting 'pepper pots' were the remains of original, octagonal finials not chimneys. The props to the gateway's infirmity did their job for some thirty years: sadly, the whole collapsed during the awful winter weather early in 1982. G.N. Kent, *c.* 1950.

32 RECTORY FARM, NORTHMOOR, OXFORDSHIRE

This 16th/17th-century timber gateway, viewed from the farmyard, stands over a track from the Rectory which crosses the right foreground here and fills the whole foreground of Pl. 20. The group photograph in Pl. 20 is taken from close to the wicket gate into St Denys' churchyard on the right here. The top of the building is a dovecote, entered by holes at first-floor level immediately above the arch. It overlooks a cattle-shed with outside steps to a loft or granary. NMR, 1979.

33 FARM, NORRIS CASTLE, EAST COWES, ISLE OF WIGHT

James Wyatt designed this model farmyard for Lord Henry Seymore in 1799. The arched, double-leaf gateway and matching doorway into the barn are, with the castellation in best farmyard Gothic, original; the wooden-shuttered silos are additions, though early examples of their type. G.B. Mason, 1949.

34 FARMYARD, BINHAM, NORFOLK

'At home, the yard affords a grateful scene'. Bloomfield, *The Farmer's Boy*

   This farmyard, dominated by the characteristic Norfolk barn with its pebble walls, contains the now nostalgic clutter which farmyards used to have – the two wagons, the two-wheeled cart with hints of other impedimenta by the cartshed to the left, the four-wheeled animal 'gang-plank', and the pigs, one stretched out in the sunlight and four with their snouts in, or very close to, the troughs. The scene is timeless yet it has gone and, in any case, as the barn's fabric shows, it was itself compound of time. H. Felton, 1945.

35 (*opposite*) CATTLE CARRIER

In the corner of another farmyard, a recognizable forerunner of the modern Landrover-pulled horse-box rests, its shafts horseless, its rooftop driver's seat empty for the moment. The cattle carrier belongs, so its rear panel informs us, to John Broomfield of North House Farm, Portslade, (East) Sussex. The five-legged tumbril or feeding-trough, standing inverted where the eye expects to see a quadruped, is surely intended as a photogenic *coup d'oeil* against the white-washed wall. The fine quality of the knapped-flint construction is better seen (*above right*) in the barn wall with the brick surrounds to its ventilation slits. H.E.S. Simmons, 1933.

36 (*overleaf*) POPLARS FARM, SHURDINGTON, GLOUCESTERSHIRE

Most of the ingredients of the pre-electricity, pre-petrol-engine farmyard are displayed here in a careful study of what is nevertheless a real scene behind the principal buildings facing away from the camera in the middle distance. The main features – dairy, barn, pig-sty, byre, waggon shed with loft, and the midden – speak for themselves, but the two-wheeled trap suggests trips four miles north-east up the road, now the A46, to Cheltenham. More prosaically, but vitally, the stack of poles clearly indicates coppicing, perhaps on the Cotswold escarpment one mile south-east along the Green Way, while the staddle-stones support the wooden base for a corn rick or similar temporary construction (*cf.* Pl. 47). Photographer unknown, *c.* 1865.

EASTWOOD MANOR FARM, EAST HARPTREE, AVON
At any moment a railway engine could puff out from under either central arch; yet it will not, for behind this farm's superbly balanced façade lies one of the most efficient, completely enclosed and covered farmyards ever constructed in England. It was completed in 1858, supposedly to the design of Robert Smith, and still works, with minor structural modifications, as the centre of a well-run, competitive modern farm. Yet the building itself has been grant-aided by the Historic Buildings Council.

The interior covers one and a half acres enclosed at a cost of £15,000. It contains, on the ground floor, two bullock yards, stalls, a dairy and stabling for eight 3-horse teams of cart-horses as well as carriage and riding horses; while beautifully dry granaries and store rooms occupy the first floor beneath the glass roof. The whole, including two fountains for the cattle and flush toilets for the workers, was supplied with running water by gravity from the Whelly stream. The basic secret of its success, however, lies underneath where lurks a gigantic, 3000-gallon slurry tank. There all is collected, and delivered thence back to the fields as manure. NMR, 1981.

37 (*opposite, above*) The main façade of the covered farmyard, illustrating its architectural unity and detail. Beneath the central steps that lead up to the granary is a roomy dog kennel; above and to either side of them are the boarded openings for the hoists to the granary.

38 (*opposite, below*) Detail of a stone-carved sheep's head let into the ashlar above the arched doorway into a side-building on the north-east of the farmyard, used as a 'sheep's hospital'.

39 (*below*) One of the two bullock yards with its original fountain; the other is through the arcade to the right. The iron columns are hollow and drain rainwater from the roof to the tank below the floor; they also support a balcony behind which, also to right, is the granary with an estimated load-carrying capacity of a ton per square yard.

40 MANOR FARM, EGHAM, SURREY

'Four ducks on a pond,
A grass-bank beyond . . .
What a little thing
To remember for years. . .'
   W. Allingham, *A Memory*

   A farmyard pond, a more traditional setting than at Eastwood Manor Farm (Pl. 39), reflects stables and barns. In front of the rear barn is another five-legged tumbril (*cf*. Pl. 35); in front of the nearer barn, the pre-war car hitched to the bale-laden trailer presumably reflects the exigencies of war-time. F. Yerbury, 1944.

41 (*opposite, below*) THE WATER CARRIER
For long after the piped water supply at Eastwood Manor Farm (Pl. 39) had provided the model for improvement, the water carrier was a familiar and indeed essential figure on many English farms. Water was needed not only for domestic purposes and for animals to drink away from the farmstead or pond but also to slake the thirst of the steam-driven traction engines increasingly used in farmyard and field.

This photograph, though unprovenanced, is likely to have been taken in Sussex. H.E.S. Simmons, 1934.

42 LONG LANE FARMHOUSE, LONG LANE, WROCKWARDINE, SHROPSHIRE
Whether distributed by pipe or barrel, water usually had to be pulled up from a lower level. The well was the traditional means of drawing water; it was often superseded by the cast-iron suction pump on farms in the 19th century. NMR, 1981.

43 MODEL DAIRY FARM, ARUNDEL CASTLE, ARUNDEL, WEST SUSSEX
'Farewell, rewards and Fairies,
Good housewives now may say,
For now foul sluts in dairies
Do fare as well as they.' Corbet, *The Fairies' Farewell*

Even less thought had been given to the flow of milk than water. A farmyard designed solely to meet the needs of dairy produce was revolutionary, a long way indeed from the windowless interior of the byre (*cf.* Pl. 76).

Here the Duke of Norfolk followed the example of the Prince Consort in constructing a new cow house with improved feed store (*background*) and an octagonal dairy for butter, cheese and syllabubs. Aristocratic dairies like this were often decorated with collections of china and tiles and some had fountains as at Frogmore and Easton (see back cover; and *cf.* Pl. 39). Photographer unknown, *c.* 1890. Copyright Duke of Norfolk.

44 CIDER PRESS, BRILLEY COURT FARM, BRILLEY, HEREFORD AND WORCESTER

In the 17th century the first cider-mill was used in Britain. Many farms had other specialized buildings or rooms around their yards, often depending on some special feature of the region's farming. In the West Country, the cider-mill-room equipped, as here, with a cider press was the local speciality. Juice from the squashed apples eventually produced an intoxicating drink, in Somerset variously called 'virgin's delight' or 'virgin's ruin'. A note on the edge of Bowen's *Map of Herefordshire* refers to that county in the mid-18th century as exceeding all others in 'Wheat, Wood, Wool, and Water but especially in Red Streak Cyder.' NMR, 1971.

45 'WOODCUTTING' NEAR WOLVERCOTE, OXFORDSHIRE

At the end of the farmyard, wood in abundance before modern materials – (*right to left*) as narrow planks for fencing, shaped for a sawing-horse, planed for a door, prepared for a lintel, sawn for logs, nailed as weatherboarding, flattened as a chopping-block, chopped for hurdling, cut for basket-making and just heaped for firewood. The most interesting features of the lady with the bow-saw are her working clothes and her concentration in holding the pose.

The photograph is in fact unprovenanced, 'near' Wolvercote being inferred from the notice announcing that 'The Mission Begins' behind her headgear. H.W. Taunt, 1901. Copyright Oxfordshire County Libraries.

46 CHURCH FARM, RUXLEY, BEXLEY, GREATER LONDON

Brick, weather-boarding, plain tiles and pantiles: here is the eastern counterpart to Langdale Farm, Devon (Pl. 27), in its reflection of locally-available materials and a different emphasis in the region's farming. The buildings shout 'arable' in their capacity to take the harvested crops while the heaped straw and much of the enclosed yard bespeak the hungry fields to which the manure will be taken.

'Church Farm' names often indicate a farm which belonged to a church; here, the barn, as is perhaps hinted by the rubble wall and buttress to the right of the door, was actually St Botolph's Church. P. Street, 1928.

47 (*overleaf, top*) THRESHING

'A fiery steam issued and came forth from behind him.' *Daniel, 7.9*

The rickyard was often close beside, rather than inside, the farmyard proper, an adjunct to the farmstead like the orchard (*right background*). As steam replaced muscle and machinery the hand, it became more common to build the ricks together in the field or next to the farmyard and thatch them, rather than heave the thousands of sheaves into barns. The harvest could then await the arrival of the traction engine and the new-fangled threshing machine to sort out chaff and straw and grain from the sheaves piled high on their hexagonal, staddle-stone platforms (*cf.* Pl. 36). Photographer unknown, *c.* 1900.

48 (*left*) TRACTOR AND PLOUGH, BIGNOR, WEST SUSSEX

It was machines like this that, in the early 20th century, began to replace the steam engine and, ultimately, the teams of horses exemplified in Pl. 25. H.E.S. Simmons, 1934.

49 (*right*) COMBINE HARVESTER AND CATERPILLAR TRACTOR, DITCHLING BEACON, EAST SUSSEX

'. . . on a half-reap'd furrow sound asleep. . .'

Keats, *To Autumn*

As the power and dominance of the internal combustion engine grew on the farm, so did the sophistication of the associated machinery. There is a logical sequence from the Barton Farm yard (Pl. 23) with its two shapely buildings to this scene in the field with its two angular machines; the task is the same. H.E.S. Simmons, 1949.

CROPS ON THE FARM

50 BARN, GUESTLING, EAST SUSSEX
The print of this very early photograph of a barn comes from a paper negative.

The barn itself, looking like something from a Constable landscape, was in a state of some dilapidation and has presumably long since disappeared like the great majority of farm buildings. Of interest is its wall for the very short length of its boards; and so too are the two different types of fencing and the gate with close-set verticals on the right. The last contrasts with the traditional five-barred gate which closed the gap on the left. Photographer unknown, *c.* 1858.

51, 52, 53 BARN, CALCOT FARM, KINGSCOTE, GLOUCESTERSHIRE

That the barn itself, though much altered and now boxed in by later buildings, is medieval in origin is suggested by the pointed window in, and the diagonal buttresses to, the gable-end. Yet there are three other pieces of 'dating' evidence: a Romano-British inscribed semicircular oolite relief, probably of an equestrian Mars with Worshippers (Pl. 52), now in the Ashmolean Museum, Oxford, but at the time of the photograph built into the barn; an inscription cut in a coign inside the south porch (Pl. 53) recording that the barn was built in 1300 by the Abbot (of Kingswood); and another incription telling us that the barn was burnt down by lightning in 1728 and rebuilt 'at the cost of Thomas Estcourt, by John Pill, carpenter', in 1729. Even when 'obvious' evidence is plentiful, dating a barn can be quite difficult. S. Pitcher, *c.* 1920s.

54 (*opposite, above*) BARN, MARLINGFORD, NORFOLK

Despite the difficulties of dating some farm buildings, it is perhaps reasonable to assume that this brick barn was built in 1666. The style of the lettering has been described as 'Artisan Mannerism'; the crowstepped gables are a mannerism of the county (*cf.* Pl. 62). H. Felton, 1951.

55 (*opposite, below*) GREAT BARRINGTON, GLOUCESTERSHIRE

This characteristic Cotswold group consists of a large barn with midstray – the double-doored porch with loft above – a wagon-shed lean-to built into the angle so formed, and a wagon shelter with round columns supporting a blind-walled granary on three huge, squared lintels. If the scene were in Sussex rather than Gloucestershire, the farmhand supporting the first column from the right might well be 'Seth lounging'. H.W. Taunt, *c.* 1895. Copyright Oxfordshire County Libraries.

56 FIRLE, EAST SUSSEX

Quite why an ox-yoke should be hanging high in the midstray of a barn is uncertain but it symbolizes the close connection between the functioning of a barn and the main contemporary source of power (*cf.* facing p.1 and Pls. 25, 46, 58). Barns were not primarily buildings *for* animals but, in coping with crops, they operated in conjunction with them.

Oxen only worked half as fast as horses but, from prehistoric times, they were the usual source of traction power on farms in England until quite recently. The ox was used regularly in Sussex until 1926, the last team being given up in 1929, so this slightly later photograph may well record the agrarian equivalent of a footballer hanging up his boots. H.E.S. Simmons, 1935.

LIBRARY
KINGSTON

57 THRESHING IN A BARN, GREAT BARRINGTON, GLOUCESTERSHIRE
Again, a Tauntian pose with a rather obviously casual arrangement of articles in the left foreground but the photograph, as intended, captures the place and circumstances in which many a farm labourer spent, and gladly through lack of other paid labour, dusty winter hours.

Flailing was usually done in teams of four or six men, rhythmically beating in rotation to four/four time. Using the flail of Biblical renown, known as the 'drashel' in the West of England, the threshers repeatedly beat a layer of cereal still on the stalk against the hard threshing floor constructed between the opposed barn doors and divided from the spaces to either side by 'mousteads'. Later, the doors would be opened to create a through-draught up into which the flailed crop would be tossed as it was winnowed, that is as grain, chaff and straw were crudely separated. Often planks or sacking were stretched across the sill during these operations to form a 'lift' or 'rack' to stop the poultry feeding on the freshly-threshed grain. Of all unlikely people, Rider Haggard recorded in 1902 'a man using a flail to thresh out beans in a barn – a very unusual sight now-a-days'; yet Hennell records the same flailing of beans in Essex, Suffolk and Cambridgeshire in 1933 and the practice has continued for 'small crops of flowers and vegetables required for pedigree seed'. H.W. Taunt, *c.* 1895. Copyright Oxfordshire County Libraries.

58 (*opposite*) STEAM ENGINE AND TITHE BARN, PILTON, SOMERSET
The technological replacement for the man with the flail, this engine, complete with stoking shovel, is in position presumably to drive another machine inside the barn. It is likely to have been a threshing machine but it might equally well have been any one of the several types of machine for chopping, mixing or separating foodstuffs that became common on late-Victorian farms.

The 14th-century barn itself is part of a grange of Glastonbury Abbey. It too (*cf.* Pl. 25) was being rethatched. Photographer and date unknown.

59 BARN, BOURNE HALL, WHERSTEAD, SUFFOLK

Rafters, purlins, collars, laithes, wall-plate, cross-rail and sill-beam, wall-posts, braces and studding – the 'bones' of the skeleton of a five-bay barn, first fitted together in this case probably about AD 1600. The timber frame rests on a brick plinth; the irregular brick nogging is unlikely to be original and contrasts with the weatherboarded gable. NMR, 1974.

60 (*opposite, below*) BARN, PRIOR'S HALL, WIDDINGTON, ESSEX
Just one of England's many magnificent medieval barn interiors exemplifies the secular counterpart of the nave and aisles of the parish church. Here the aisle-posts rest on sills laid across the floor of the aisles themselves, emphasizing the division of the lengthy interior into eight bays. They provide convenient storage units for what are probably swedes (*right*) and sacks (*left*), while the nave itself, instead of holding crops, houses vehicles which carry and process them. RCHM, 1916.

61 BARN, OLD HALL FARM, OVER KELLET, LANCASHIRE
This example of a barn from a farm in north-western England contrasts with the preceding nine from the south. There is a crop-storage element open to the roof (*right*), inside the high but curiously narrow entrance, and (*left*) there is a characteristic arrangement of stable and loft or granary approached by external stairs (*cf.* Pl. 11). NMR, 1968.

62 BARN, HALES HALL, HALES, NORFOLK

Another of the great (late) medieval barns of England, this time in brick, this East Anglian example with its characteristic crow-stepped gables forms the southern side of what was the outer court, still extant and with its impressive gatehouse on the north, of a moated house beyond the barn's further end. It is 184 feet long. Built by Sir James Hobart who became Henry VII's Attorney General, the complex flourished in the 16th century but was much reduced by the early 18th century after the Catholic family had experienced difficulties in the 17th century. It is now being tended again.

The unusual chimney appears to be original, serving domestic quarters for farm staff in the three nearest bays marked by windows. NMR, 1961.

63 (*opposite*) BARN, THE PRIORY, LATTON, ESSEX

A genuine 'priory barn', for the barn has been created out of the ruins of the early-14th-century crossing of the Priory Church, originally founded in the 12th century for Austin Canons and abandoned by 1534. The view, from the north-west, shows the remains of the north transept (*left*), the crossing (*centre*) and (*right*) the eastern end of the nave walls with the weathering of the roof of the former aisle and a circular clerestorey window. The walls are of flint-rubble with dressings of Roman brick and Reigate stone. Interesting farmyard touches include the double-leafed barn door in the centre of the nave and the iron cauldron chocking the end of the gate in the centre. Under the crossing at the time of the photograph were a waggon, seed drill and corn-binder. RCHM, 1921.

64 BARN, OAK HOUSE FARM, HAMPSTEAD NORRIS, BERKSHIRE

This open-sided and open-ended barn consists only of an impressive thatched roof, an elementary frame and a floor supported by joists linking ten pairs of staddle-stones. The central bay does not have a raised floor and was presumably driven through by carts. The 'crop' here is baled straw after threshing. Together with the weight of the roof, the total load on the stones must have been considerable, as indeed their disposition at the far end suggests.

The type, now rare, originated in the 16th century and became popular throughout southern England in the 18th century. NMR, 1967.

65 (*opposite, below*) GRANARY, BARTON TURF, NEATISHEAD, NORFOLK
Recently renovated as a 'unique holiday home', the further enticing description of this 18th-century wherry arch as a 'unique waterside building' hardly does justice to its essential nature; for it spans, and not merely rests beside, the water. Its situation and design were chosen deliberately so that it could load and unload wares, and specifically grain, into and from the local type of boat called a wherry. The central window can be seen to have been inserted into a blocked opening, immediately beside the bottom corners of which are the tell-tale put-log holes for the pulley. Herbert Felton, 1948.

66 CORN-DRYING KILN, DOLLERLINE, ASKERTON, CUMBRIA
'I hate that dreadful hollow behind the little wood'. Tennyson, *Maud*
   Even if here it looks plain uninteresting rather than 'dreadful', this hollowed mound is the remains of a probably 17th-century corn-drying kiln. It represents what was once a quite common feature on farms, particularly in the north, and one which marked a crucial stage in the conversion of the harvest into food. Other types of kiln have characterized the farmed landscape at different times and in different regions. RCHM, 1970.

67 SILO, THE NODE DAIRY AND STUD, CODICOTE, HERTFORDSHIRE
This remarkable composition, standing boldly somewhere between the Brothers Grimm and Trinity House, was designed by Maurice Chesterton in 1927. The thatched lighthouse is actually a heavily disguised silo (*cf.* Pl. 33), a serious type of building for converting grass into silage (*cf.* also outside back cover). NMR, 1981.

68 (*opposite*) OASTHOUSE, HOPE FARM, SNARGATE, KENT
The oast, another specialist farm building, was for drying hops to make beer. This type was developed by John Read of Horsmonden, Kent, in the late 18th century. An earlier, local improver in matters agrarian had been Thomas à Becket who had been much involved in land drainage hereabouts in the 12th century. F.J. Palmer, 1956.

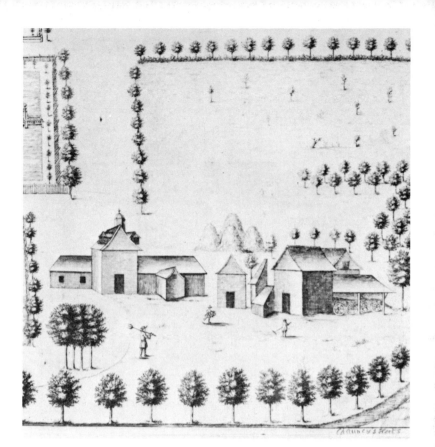

69, 70 FARM AND MILL, BUSHEY HALL, BUSHEY, HERTFORDSHIRE
These two drawings from Chauncey's *Antiquities of Hertfordshire* (1700) are roughly contemporary with at least the use of many of the buildings in this book; and they both summarize and anticipate points made and still to come. The layout, buildings and other features of the farmstead, such as the haycocks forming a rickyard (Pl. 69), anticipate aspects of photography which did not begin to record similar scenes for a century and a half; while the mill (Pl. 70) represents all those other buildings and structures dotted around the countryside, vital to farming but not necessarily in farmsteads. NMR, 1976. Copyright Hertford Museum.

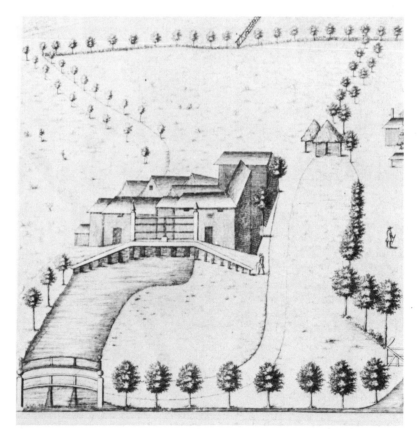

71 (*overleaf*) WHITE MILL, SHAPWICK, DORSET
'What, man! More water glideth by the mill
Than wots the miller of.'

> Shakespeare, *Titus Andronicus*

In arable areas, all roads led, sooner or later, to the corn-mill. Its central importance in the farming cycle was recognized in medieval times by the difficulty anyone experienced who tried to have their harvest ground other than at the manorial mill. New power sources, railways and lorries put an end to that.

This mill, water-powered and beside the miller's house, has an archway over the millrace with a keystone dated 1776 and two desirable detached dovecotes (*cf.* Pls. 90-5) overlooking the mill pond in its idyllic setting. Photographer unknown, *c.* 1900.

72 WINDMILL, SAXSTEAD GREEN, SUFFOLK
After muscle and water-power, the wind was another source of energy for the farm in the days before various
engines and machines became available. The windmills, though now such an attractive feature of the English
landscape and so beloved by conservationists, illustrate how that source was applied to what remained one of the
basic tasks of the agrarian way of life – the conversion of cereal crop to food.

Windmills were built in various ways: this is a post-mill and was first referred to in 1706, when the miller was
Amos Webber. It has not worked since early this century but is maintained as a Guardianship monument. M. Wright,
c. 1950s.

73 (*opposite, above*) WHEELHOUSE AND BARN, HOLLY FARM, HOOTON ROBERTS, SOUTH YORKSHIRE
Muscle-power could be more effectively used if transmitted through more efficient machines. The application of this
principle to farming in the late 18th and early 19th centuries led, *inter alia,* to these singular-looking polygonal,
circular or, sometimes rectangular buildings being added to many barns. Their names vary locally: gin-gang, gin-
house, horse-gear, track-shed, wheel-rig, wheelhouse are examples. Their function was to provide a covered but
ventilated space in which a horse, by walking round and round a machine to which it was attached, could power
through a simple system of shafts and cogs another machine which was threshing, grinding or otherwise doing
things to crops in the barn. The building represents exactly the equine equivalent of Pls. 57 and 58, and another
attempt to apply energy to exactly the same task.

The barn itself, probably 18th century and three storeys high, provides an interesting visual forerunner of the huge
building in Pl. 30. NMR, 1975.

74 POTATO-PLANTING MACHINE

'An attachment à la Plato for a bashful young
potato . . .' W.S. Gilbert, *Patience*

Not all farming tasks easily lent themselves to
mechanization; not all machines led to *the*
technological break-through.

The gloom and apprehension apparent among
the crew of this brand-new, nine-cylinder, bi-
pedal 'stretched' jumbo wheelbarrow, snapped
here before departure from the safety of the
kitchen garden for the ploughed fields outside, is
perhaps symbolized by the single brick propping
up the further leg. H.W. Taunt, *c.* 1900. Copyright
Oxfordshire County Libraries.

LIVESTOCK ON THE FARM

75 COWSHED, HOME FARM, DONINGTON HALL, HEREFORD AND WORCESTER
Cow W15 (or 51M?) in its farmstead habitat: a typical timber-framed and (later) brick, open-fronted cowshed with (hay) loft over, giving on to a completely enclosed cattle-yard deep in maturing manure. The building is the west Midlands equivalent of that on the left of Pl. 27. NMR, 1970.

76 (*opposite*) BYRE, LLANYBLODWEL, SHROPSHIRE
The cowhouse, byre, shippon or milking-shed is one of the main buildings on a pastoral or mixed farm, as essential as the barn on an arable farm. Characteristic internal fittings include at least one row of stalls, each stall for one or two cows, tethering arrangements in the stalls, and some sort of drainage system. Internal lighting was often poor; access to a midden was important, though the door was usually wide enough for but one cow at a time.

   Here, the far end of the building appears to be a loose-box, probably for sick or pregnant cows; the roof structure is probably of the 17th century but much of the timber throughout is re-used – see, for example, the empty tenon-holes, – the walls have been raised and the roof has been reconstructed. G.B. Mason, 1961.

77 PIGSTIES, CHURCH FARM, SANDIACRE, DERBYSHIRE

Pigsties used to be common on farms, and at the homes of the farm-workers too, for the pig was the most available source of domestic meat, at least in the countryside, until this century. From the single sty to the battalion-like regularity of the properly built piggery (Pls. 30, 93), the architecture varies widely, but little of it can be as 'natural' as here where the porcine accommodation is carved out of the living rock. NMR, 1973.

78 FARMYARD, NORTH HINKSEY, OXFORDSHIRE

'. . . a jewel of gold in a swine's snout' (*Proverbs*, 22) may seem unlikely in these characteristic but unnatural circumstances; the pigs, however, were sufficiently in their seventh heaven to stand still long enough, amazingly in the light of other Taunt studies, for the photographer to take what must nevertheless have been a snap by his usual standards.

    Again, stone barn wall and iron braces apart, the 'organic-ness' of the scene predominates, as it always has done in lowland England (*cf.* Pl. 29). The splendid thatched tumbril here offers an alternative interpretation of the sets of 'four-posters' reconstructed as granaries at 'Little Woodbury'. H.W. Taunt, *c.* 1900. Copyright Oxfordshire County Libraries.

79 (*opposite, above*) STABLES, HOPE FARMHOUSE, SNARGATE, KENT

'. . . the stables are the real centre of the household'. Shaw, *Heartbreak House*
In pre-internal combustion days, the stables were also the equivalent of the later garage, essential for farming tasks both serious and sporting; but they do not seem to inspire either great photographs or interesting-looking buildings.

    This is a fairly typical stable block of the 19th century, dull but with enough detail to indicate that on the whole horses were better looked after than contemporary cows. F.J. Palmer, 1956.

80 'STABLE', COLVILLE HALL, WHITE RODING, ESSEX

This magnificent early-16th-century building is yet another in the same farmyard as illustrated in Pl. 24, and if it were indisputably a stable in origin then it would be a worthy example of that sort of building to exist in the Colville context – 'an exquisite piece of its type' (Pevsner). Clearly the ground floor had been a stable for a long time when the photograph was taken but only the central door looks original and it is difficult to visualize horses climbing the steps to the other. The brick nogging is also at least partly secondary (*cf.* Pl. 59). The jettied first floor, with its range of five unglazed windows, was occupied by a single chamber, perhaps feastroom or manorial courtroom, entered by an original ladderstair from the stable range below. As a stable, whether originally so or not, it is a very fine example indeed, especially when compared with the typical stable range in Pl. 79. RCHM, 1921.

81 STABLES, CHURCH FARM, FRESSINGFIELD, SUFFOLK

'. . . from the hag-ridden magic and enchanted woods of Celtic antiquity'. Lloyd George

Even the high esteem in which horses are often held is hardly likely to have equipped a stable with this great moulded beam, yet here are all the accoutrements of a stable: the eating trough, the drinking trough, the hayrack and the bales of straw (the calves trying to get in on the act are in an adjacent building and irrelevant). This is indeed a stable but it has been fashioned inside a 14th-century hall-house of some consequence.

Yet the feature of greatest interest is the flint hanging from a peg driven into the beam. This is a 'hag-stone'. The word 'hag' is used here exactly as by Macbeth – 'How now, you secret, black and midnight hags?' A little later, John Aubrey recorded what we see here: 'To hinder the Night Mare they hang on a String a Flint with a hole in it (naturally) by the manger . . . It is to prevent the Night Mare *viz.* the Hag from riding the Horses who will sometimes sweat at Night. The Flint thus hung does hinder it'.

So deeply embedded is this tradition in English rural life that it has given us at least three common words and/or phrases: 'nightmare', 'hag-ridden' and 'all of a sweat'. The flint with the natural hole seems to represent the All-Seeing Eye; its function was to ward off the ghostly Mare whose night visitation, as well as making the real horse sweat, brought intimations of death. George Ewart Evans writes well about this in *The Pattern Under the Plough,* chaps. 18 and 19. NMR, 1966.

82 SMITHY, COLYTON, DEVON

It was unusual for the ordinary farm to have its own smithy though there was one at Eastwood Manor Farm, just to the left of Pl. 37, and quite often one for a whole estate. Here the blacksmith works from the village street, shoeing carthorses that were still working despite the rubber tyres and bus timetable to the right – and the date of the photograph. Smiths, like shepherds (*cf.* Pl. 83), do not seem to have generated a particular architecture or type of building. A.W. Everett, *c.* 1950. Copyright A.W. Everett.

Sheep and shepherding, together in many ways the basis of a great deal in English farming, hardly seem to require any buildings at all; yet the wealth created by sheep farming has littered the landscape with fine architecture and substantial structures.

83 SHEPHERD AND SHEEP, WINTER'S DOWN, HAMPSHIRE
'I like to look at the winding of a great down, with two or three numerous flocks of sheep on it...'
Cobbet, *Rural Rides*
  The shepherd is Mr Frank Cozens; his tools are his crook, stick and dog. The hurdling, used at lambing time for protection, at dipping time for collection (*cf.* Pl. 2), and in autumn and spring for folding the flock on the arable to dung it (as here?), is as much as sheep needed in the way of 'buildings' on the chalk downs of southern England. H.E.S. Simmons, 1933.

84 (*opposite, above*) SHEPHERD'S HUT, CROWMARSH, OXFORDSHIRE
A nervous young shepherd recorded with rather touching honesty: 'I was so young, that I dursn't stay out in the dark by myself. I was not man enough to stay with the flock throughout the night; so for a little while my father used to come out with me at night and sleep in the little ol' cabin along o' me. But I soon got used to it by myself and I took no notice of the queer little noises you hear in the night.' P.S. Spokes, 1971.

85 SHEEP SHEARING, WITNEY, OXFORDSHIRE
Tusser advises in *June Husbandrie*:
. . .shear him, and spare not, at two days an end,
the sooner the better his corps will amend.

Reward not they sheep, when ye take off his coat,
with twitches and patches as broad as a groat;
Let no such engentleness happen to thine,   Gentils were maggots.
lest fly with the gentils do make it to pine.   H.W. Taunt, *c.* 1900. Copyright Oxfordshire County Libraries.

86 THE HAY FIELD, YARNTON, OXFORDSHIRE
'So *that's* what hay looks like'. Queen Mary

   Of course this is posed, like much of Taunt's other work, but no more so than the 'action' photographs of politicians and personalities of today's newspapers; and here is recorded, at its annual enactment, a genuine historical tradition dating at least from the time of Domesday Book. References to 'meadow' are frequent in the entries of the 1086 Survey. '40 acres' of it are recorded then, for example, in the same Laxton depicted 550 years later on the manorial map from which Pl.10 is an extract. That map shows every dole, or share, of grassland in the meadows, just like the strips in the common arable fields. The 130 acres of common meadows constituted about one-tenth of the ploughlands; they were mown in strips in later June/July by men using two-handled scythes and the hay was raked into cocks, ready for carting, by both men and women. On the 1 August, the hayfields were opened for common grazing which continued until 1 November; or, as the by-laws in 1686 expressed rather more eloquently: 'It is pained that the pinders shall pinn out of they Medowes after the first of Nov: next in paine of their not so doing 10s.'.

   The horses, carts, double-handed scythes and strips of hay of the Yarnton scene perpetuate elements of the long tradition lying behind the early-twentieth-century formalities of allocating the hay amongst the villagers with rights in the common fields.

The 'lots' of the three fields were distributed by the method of drawing balls of which there were thirteen, named Perry, Harry, Dunn, White, Freeman, Green, Rother, Boulton, Gilbert, Boat, Water Molley, Water Geoffrey and William of Bladon. Each represents mowing rights to whole, half or quarter strips of field and to commons of pasture for one cow or bullock per acre or for one horse per two acres. That mowing had already taken place is a little disconcerting: had Taunt arrived too late?

The lady in the photograph would be expected to make the draw assisted by two farmers (meadsmen), one of whom is holding the bag containing the balls.

The decision whether or not to wear a jacket and/or necktie, heavy with social significance, must have been a delicate one. The manifest sartorial nuances, in a scene surely only self-conscious because of the camera's presence, mirror in the field the more blatant gradations of the same society at play (Pl.20). But blatant too is the absence here of Yarnton's young and able-bodied men in the year of Passchendaele. H.W. Taunt, 1917. Copyright Oxfordshire County Libraries.

87 (*opposite*) 'BRIDGE WITH MOWER AND MAN', GUITING POWER OR GUITING TEMPLE, GLOUCESTERSHIRE

A fine, nostalgic study, Gray-like in its elegaic rusticity, it serves here to emphasize the importance of meadow and its proper harvesting for hay in the mixed farming economy of the Cotswolds. Nevertheless, by 1895 the 'mower' or double-handed scythe was becoming somewhat anachronistic as a tool in general use, for the horse-drawn mowing machine, as seen left of centre in Pl. 86, was introduced in the late 1850s. H.W. Taunt, *c.* 1895. Copyright Oxfordshire County Libraries.

88 CUTTING THE HAYSTACK, BUNCTON, WEST SUSSEX

After cutting, the grass in the hayfield dries to become hay and is then stacked. The haystack is thatched to keep out rain and fenced to keep out grazing animals; the hay is compressed under its own weight and is then used up as necessary as animal feed during the winter and spring.

   Here the stack has been cut vertically into 'desses' and the hay is being removed truss by truss. The layering in the stack is clearly visible. The horse and cart are either just to transport the cutter or a small amount of hay. H.E.S. Simmons, 1937.

89 HUNTINGDON WARREN, LYDFORD, DEVON
This remarkable landscape, lying high on Dartmoor between 1250 and 1500 feet above sea level, is apparently being invaded by maggot-like objects crawling up the hill slope from the two streams. The 'maggots' are oblong mounds with narrow side or surrounding ditches, deliberately built as rabbit warrens. Significantly, they are located at the furthest corner of the parish, the boundary of which runs along the valley from the right and up the valley left of centre. The parishioners were not being kind to rabbits in providing them with a home; rather were they providing themselves with a meat larder, a walk away but always available, weather allowing, and doubtless a welcome if occasional complement to the sparse meat element in their diet. A successful warren could also be profitable.

The warren, which is of medieval date, is mixed up with features of both earlier and later landscapes. The second millennium BC, when this area would have been good farming country, is represented by the burial cairn (*right centre*), the roundish settlement enclosures (*bottom left* and *centre*) and by numerous hut circles. Field enclosures range in date, probably, from them to (*bottom right*) the 19th century. There is also evidence of industry – mining and tin-streaming – with the landscape scored across the centre by a leat cutting both prehistoric and medieval farming features. West Air Photography, 1975. Copyright West Air Photography.

90 (*opposite*) COCKPIT, THE GRANGE, WOOLAVINGTON, SOMERSET
Hen-coops, like sheep pens, do not often compel photographic inspiration (*cf.* Pl. 23) so the sporting side of poultry life is represented here. This thatched cylindrical building was used as a cockpit but was it built as such? – its height and diameter of 14 feet hardly suggest so and neither does its medieval buttresses. Could it have been a dovecote at first? NMR, 1980.

91 DOVECOTE, LUNTLEY COURT, DILWYN, HEREFORD AND WORCESTER
Pigeons, like rabbits, were kept for meat and of course they also laid eggs; but, unlike rabbits, their needs created a distinct type of building, the dovecote. Many survive associated with their farm and Luntley Court provides a good example. The farmhouse is dated 1674. A similar pairing exists at Dormston in the same county, where the buildings are dated 1667. In both cases the dovecotes are characterized by their weatherings. Not that pigeon-farming was necessarily so peacefully innocent: early in the 17th century, saltpetre extracted from pigeon droppings had been used in the manufacture of gunpowder. B.T. Clayton, *c.* 1920s. Copyright B.T. Batsford.

92 DOVECOTE, MANOR FARM, BAGINTON, WARWICKSHIRE
Another four-square dovecote, this one contrasts with that in Pl. 91 in its stone structure and somewhat later date. The rather elaborate entrance façade facing the camera calls into question whether the building was solely a dovecote – why should it have a chimney if so? Perhaps the ground floor served other purposes; perhaps the Edwardian gentleman, clearly introduced to the scene to give a melancholy human interest, could have told us what they were. F.T.S. Houghton, *c.* 1910.

93 DOVECOTE, CHILLINGTON HALL, BOWOOD, STAFFORDSHIRE
Contrasting with the rusticity of the last two examples, this dovecote sits fairly and octagonally in a farmyard with barn, byre and stables behind and waggon-sheds and piggeries to either side. The ornate cupola and circular dormer windows with diagonal latticing might now be considered a little pretentious for mere pigeons but were doubtless very fashionable when constructed *c.* 1730. H. Felton, 1962.

95 (*below*) DOVECOTE, HARLYN,
ST MERRYN, CORNWALL
Dovecotes come in many shapes and sizes.
Here eggs and birds must have been collected
from the outside since the fifty or so nests are
arranged around a solid central column of
masonry. H. Felton, 1954.

94 (*above*) DOVECOTE, WYTHAM, OXFORDSHIRE
Round, square or polygonal, these dovecotes were hollow inside with nesting-boxes
arranged in serried ranks around their walls. Eggs, and birds, were usually taken
from a centrally-pivotted revolving ladder except in square interiors like this where
vertical ladders would have been necessary.

   Having supplementary eggs and meat on the farm provided a welcome change for
the dovecote owners but the other side of the equation for those living off the land is
recalled in the country jingle about planting seeds:
'One for the pigeon, one for the crow,
One to rot and one to grow.' P.S. Spokes, 1962.

FARMS IN THE LANDSCAPE

Former fields, long-forgotten tracks, settlements which have disappeared – they all still exist in the landscape, sometimes visibly as an archaeological site, sometimes less obviously as an ancient feature incorporated into today's farmland, and sometimes invisibly except to the skilled gaze of the aerial observer. But the past is always there, partly influencing the present, whether our chosen farms in England are to the east and mainly crop-producing or to the west and mainly stock-keeping. NMR, 1970s.

96 GOSBERTON, LINCOLNSHIRE
The modern farm sits symmetrically with its large, enclosed rectilinear fields containing, at ground level, no vestige of antiquity; yet in reality it is surrounded by a complex series of ancient landscapes. The sinuous dark lines are of former water-courses, probably post-Roman. In the same area are many thinner lines of the Roman landscape.

97 BATWORTHY, CHAGFORD, DEVON
An expanding, present-day farm with its now-hedged small enclosed fields assarted in medieval times from the Moor is approached by a single track. It kinks round a prehistoric farm, known as the Round Pound, runs parallel to a prehistoric track and crosses the boundaries of fields laid out in a planned rectilinear system 3/4000 years ago.

INDEX

Roman numerals refer to the pages of introduction; Arabic numbers refer to the plates.